My Moms and Me!

Jessica L. Ibarra

This book is dedicated to the millions of adults who as children, lacked acceptance and representation. This book is also dedicated to the millions of children, who will see love as love and be a positive change in the world.

To my Life Partner and Best Friend.
Thank you for giving me all of your love and support. My love for you is immense.

To my Mom & Dad.
Thank you for showing me unconditional LOVE.

Today I woke up happy, as happy as can be, because I have two moms who love and care for me!

Mom helps me get dressed, and teaches me how to brush. She knows I am normally in a hurry, and teaches me not to rush.

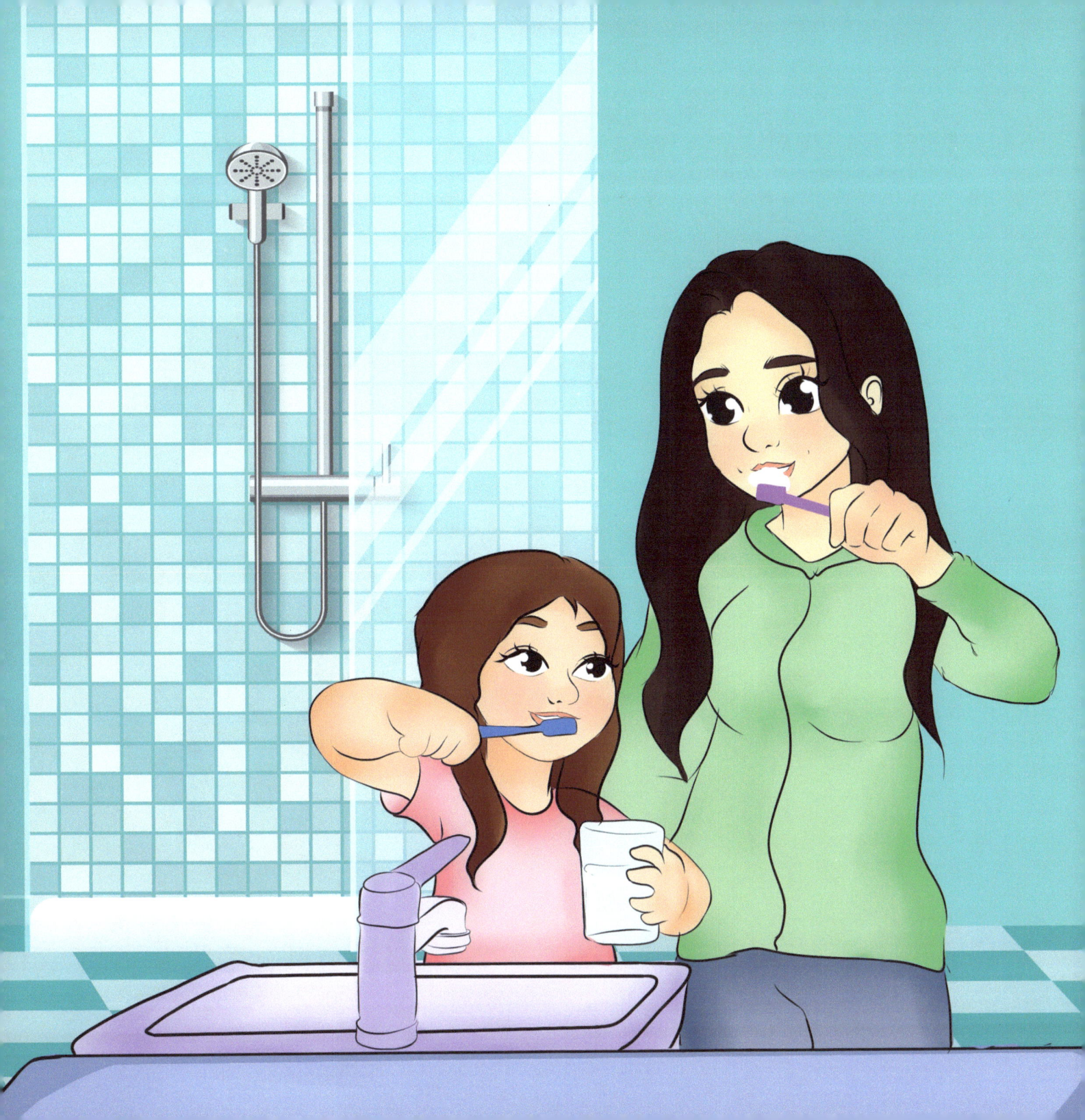

One of my favorites is when we all cook together, just us 3, my mommies and me!

Mom knows all of my favorite foods and teaches me how to measure.

Eating what we made together gives me such great pleasure!

Today I woke up happy, as happy as can be, because I have two moms who love and care for me!

After breakfast we head outside to get some air.

Mom says "Hold on chickie first, let's teach you how to fix that hair."

Mom asks me how I would like it styled.

I said today, I am feeling something fun and a little wild.
She shows me how to part and tie up my hair.
Then gives me two cute, little, purple bows to wear.

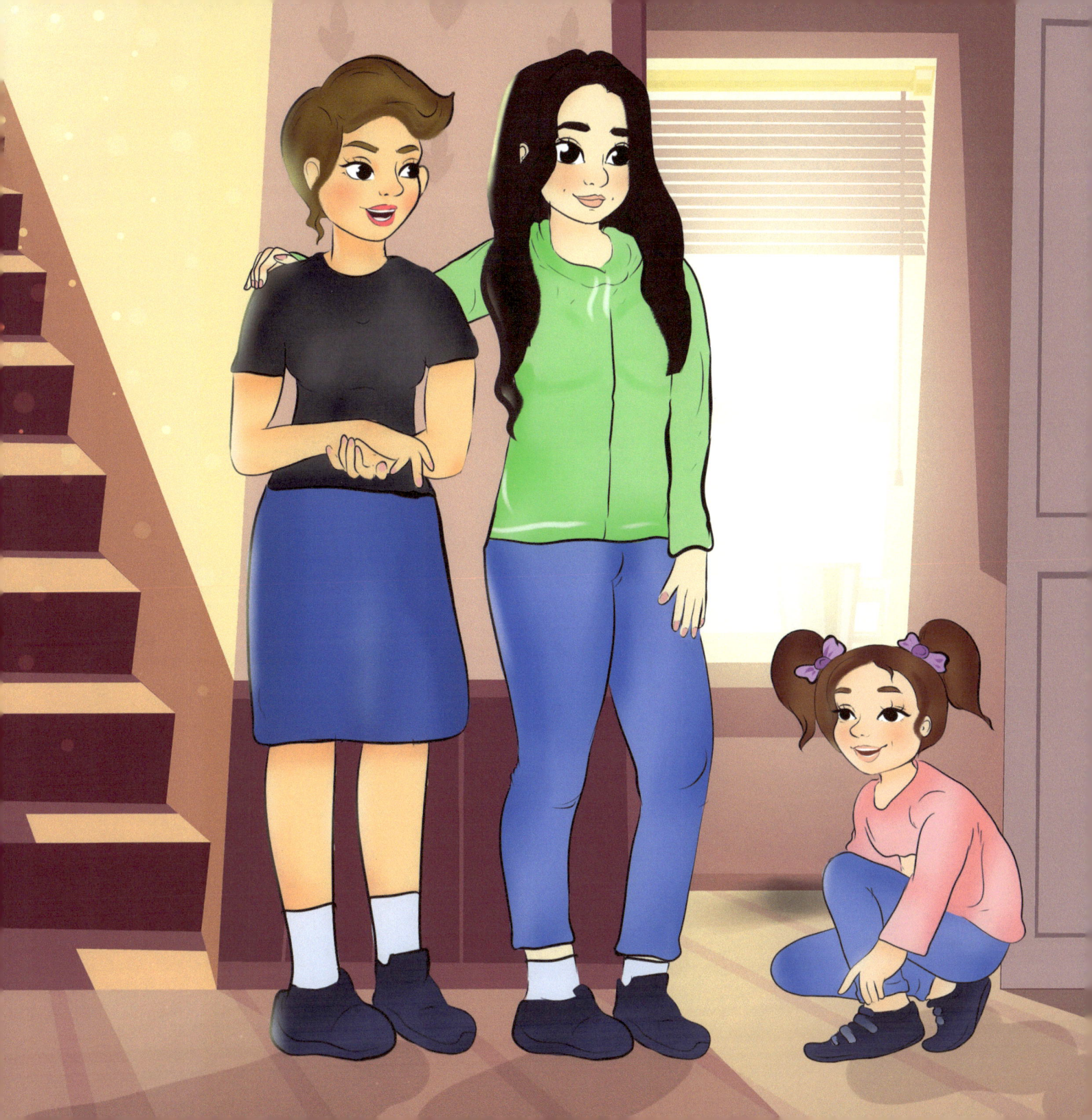

Once all finished we go outside to have a soccer pass.

Then spend time looking for little critters in the tall grass.

We spent the whole day outside, we even saw a Queen bee!
We had such a great time playing, just my moms and me.

The sun starts to set, so I know it's almost time for dinner.
We race back inside, and guess what? I'm the WINNER!

We wash up, set the table, and get ready to eat.
It all smells oh so delicious, I jump right in my seat!

We say Thank you for the food, each and every night.
So much to be thankful for, everything in sight!

Today I woke up happy, as happy as can be, because I have two moms who love and care for me!

They help me with my schoolwork, and teach me how to read.
We even make up fun sing-along songs and take turns singing the lead.

Once finished all my studying, it's time to wash up for bed.
Snuggled up in my PJ's with a book that cannot wait to be read.
Tonight I go to sleep happy, as happy as can be, because I have two moms who love and care for me!

About the Author

Jessica Ibarra is a native to the Philadelphia, Pennsylvania area. As a natural caretaker and teacher of children, as well as an active member of the LGBT community, Jessica first hand experienced the lack of material that positively depicts healthy and happy queer relationships. Jessica's mission is to continue to create stories that brining families together and show many different examples of love.